Tilly the Goat Princess was written accidentally. I had intended on writing a little story about Tilly to help promote the caramel that we make. And a friend of mine said "Do you realize that you just wrote a children's story". So that was the start of our adventure.

Please check out our website www.sugarnannys.com. Tilly and I would like to THANK YOU for supporting the AMERICAN FARMER.

With Love,
Pamela Slabaugh

AuthorHouse™
1663 Liberty Drive
Bloomington, IN 47403
www.authorhouse.com
Phone: 833-262-8899

Because of the dynamic nature of the Internet, any web addresses or links contained in this book may have changed
since publication and may no longer be valid. The views expressed in this work are solely those of the author and do not
necessarily reflect the views of the publisher, and the publisher hereby disclaims any responsibility for them.

Any people depicted in stock imagery provided by Getty Images are models,
and such images are being used for illustrative purposes only.
Certain stock imagery © Getty Images.

This book is printed on acid-free paper.

ISBN: 978-1-4817-2181-3 (sc)
       978-1-4817-2180-6 (e)

Library of Congress Control Number: 2013903958

Print information available on the last page.

Published by AuthorHouse 04/20/2021

authorHOUSE®

Chantilly Lace is Tilly's real name. Sometimes I refer to her as Tilly Willy which she really does not like.

Tilly is a well bred fancy Saanen Dairy Goat.

Registered

#1ST

1

ADGA

SAANEN Grand Champion

Miss Tilly's Dream

Sandra Stephens

Tilly has the
personality of a
REAL Glamour girl

Tilly is very
graceful Tilly does
not walk she struts

and when she runs,
which she really
prefers not to, she runs
like she has stiletto
heels on

and oh she HATES
to have her coat
wind-blown.

Sandra Stephens

9

When the weather is questionable she
either pushes some other goat out the
door to check the weather or

she might peak out.
She HATES snow
and is not fond of
the rain

Tilly does not like her coat messed up.

Tilly was born in Georgia and really is a GRITS.
(Goats raised in the South)

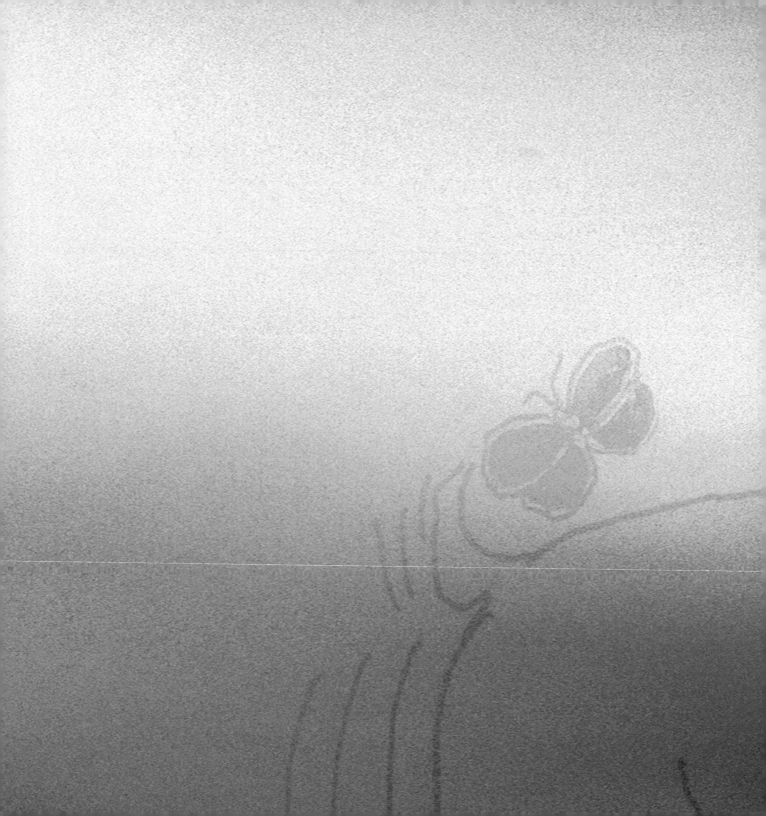

Draw Your Own Tilly!

Tickl Tilly with Color!

Printed in the United States
by Baker & Taylor Publisher Services